how to

be a

media

darling

Karen Jayne Blattenbauer

TABLE OF CONTENTS

INTRODUCTION

Hello, friend! I'm glad you're here.

By the end of this book, I hope it feels as if we are old friends talking about public relations, growing your business, and celebrating all your media successes.

Because you invested in this PR resource, there's a good chance you want to strategically grow your brand's reputation. You're not here to become wildly famous overnight. You want to learn how to grab and maintain the right kind of attention to grow your brand.

While having tons of media attention is appealing—and I totally hope you get there—the thing I hear from most entrepreneurs like you are:

- You want to have more coverage and attention from the media for your efforts.
- You want to create compelling content that truly sets your brand a part.

- You want your publicity efforts to attract your ideal client. In droves.

To all three of these I say yes, yes, yes! These are the most important things you want when you're laying out your publicity strategy. I promise, you'll go farther with the well-planned PR steps outlined in this book than with thousands of spur-of-the-moment pitches, posts, or tactics.

That's what we'll be focusing on throughout this book.

I'm going to help you define your PR goals.

I'm going to help you understand who you're truly pitching.

And I'm going to show you real-world examples of brands who are doing their own PR really well.

Which may have a few of you wondering, "Well, who are you?"

I'm Karen Jayne Blattenbauer. But you can call me KJ.

I'm an expert at public relations, who has nearly 25 years of experience in both agency and corporate settings.

I'm originally from a small town in North Dakota, so I know first-hand all publicity isn't good publicity. Plus, I know the right ways to spin any news to get attention.

My happiest days are spent championing the underdog and helping entrepreneurs like you receive the recognition your dreams deserve.

I'm passionate about sharing the advice, ideas, and tools that will bring your success. Which is why I'm so passionate about this book. If you follow the steps in this book, you will become a media darling and learn how to prep for and secure your own press.

But, even if some chapters seem more appealing than others, make sure you go in order. There's a method to my madness here, and applying the lessons in their intended order will help you perfect the perfect PR foundation.

Remember when I said you'll go farther with well-planned PR steps that clearly communicate what your brand is about? Buckle up, friend! The PR party is about to get started and I cannot wait to see you inside the rest of this book.

Ready to get after it? You've got this.

CHAPTER ONE
WHAT IS PR

By definition, public relations is the art of convincing an audience—outside your usual circle of influence—to promote your idea, purchase your product, support your position, or recognize your accomplishments.

When you get down to it, public relations is simply how you tell your unique brand story through coverage in newspapers, magazines, online publications, and on radio and TV.

For free.

Whether they refer to it as public relations, PR, or publicity, public relations is how today's brands are getting their message in front of their best clients and potential customers through activities like press releases, media pitches, hosting events, blogging, and managing influencers.

At its best, PR is a third-party endorsement from reputable media outlets that your brand is the go-to in your niche.

In fact, PR is the support function necessary to make conversations—especially social media ones—relevant, effective, and engaging with your target audience.

If you're new to PR, it may feel overwhelming to think about mastering all the promotional tactics that can be used. But don't worry, this book will totally get you up to speed.

If you're not new to PR, please continue reading. In this chapter, I'll explain my take on PR and set the groundwork for the rest of this book.

While PR may consist of a variety of different tactics, they all work together to create a foundation for your business: attracting your target audience, nurturing relationships, and making offers your dream customers will appreciate and respond to.

Let's take a closer look at how that happens, shall we?

HOW PR WORKS

In many ways, PR is no different than traditional advertising.

In both, smart brands seek to develop mutually-beneficial relationships with their target audience.

But PR has more credibility than traditional advertising because it is designed to reach your target audience through tactics that don't require you to pay for them.

For example, think about the last important purchase you made. Perhaps you purchased a new camera, hired someone to walk your dog, or changed up the location for your monthly girls-only happy hour.

Regardless of what it was, you probably began by searching the Internet or social media to learn more about available options, who provided them, and what your best solutions were.

Your ultimate buying decision was then based on the reviews you read, feedback from friends or family, and the options, features, and pricing you researched, plus if said solution appeared in any reputable media outlets.

Most purchasing decisions begin online, but end with credible, third-party endorsements.

That being the case, a positive reputation and online presence is absolutely necessary—regardless of what you have to offer.

The key is to develop a PR strategy that puts you in all the places your target audience is already hanging out, then using a variety of PR tactics to connect with them back to your brand.

This could include PR tactics like:
- Generating informative and educational blog content to keep your target audience updated on the latest industry news, how it impacts them, and how you can solve any problems that may arise as a result of the industry updates.
- Crafting news-worthy and relevant media pitches that have media outlets standing in lining waiting to cover your brand in their latest TV segment, blog, or magazine.
- Sharing social media content that not only engages them in relevant conversation, but their friends and followers as well.
- Distributing press releases that announce your latest offerings, big wins, and events to keep your target audience aware of what you've been up to.

- Acquiring a consistent stream of reputable, third-party endorsements from both the media and industry influencers to show your target audience you're the industry expert.

THE BENEFITS OF PR

The benefits of having a strategic publicity plan are numerous; however, a few of my very favorites include:
- Making it easier to generate brand awareness so yours is always top of mind
- Helping you build awareness and credibility with both new and potential customers
- Protecing and managing your brand's image
- Kickstarting word-of-mouth and social sharing—plus the benefits that come with these
- Shortening the sales cycle by communicating the right message to the right people

When you put all these PR pieces together strategically, you end up with an efficient, easy-to-implement plan. And, while it may seem intimidating to build that plan from scratch, it's as simple as learning and integrating one PR tactic at a time—to reap some pretty huge and awesome benefits.

Which is why I've put together this step-by-step guide on how to properly perform PR just for you. To help you build or refine your own publicity plan without any false starts or missteps that come with doing it alone.

PR BY THE NUMBERS

Wise people say there is power in numbers and that holds true with PR.

While you've probably heard of brands having success with one-off press hits that lead to mass sales, for most business owners, a single article isn't going to make you millions.

However, a steady stream of media coverage will help you build credibility, influence, and brand awareness.

If PR is more of a marathon than a sprint, you may be wondering why you should bother. Here are a few figures for you to mull over.

Cost of a full-page advertisement in a regional newspaper
Approximately $3,000 based on rate card pricing

Hiring a public relations agency at a modest rate
Approximately $24,000 annually or $2,000 per month

Cost of a full-page advertisement in a national newspaper
Starting at $75,000 based on rate card pricing

Cost of receiving coverage in the press
$0

In addition to being easy on the budget as noted above, media coverage also is better for your brand. A media outlet choosing to feature your brand because they believe their audience will be interested in what you have to offer versus you paying to get placement will provide you with far more credibility.

PR ISN'T ROCKET SCIENCE

If you're short on time, it can be tempting to hire out your publicity needs to a PR professional or agency. The truth is, no matter how good the PR consultant and firm you hire is, they'll never be able to learn, know, or promote your business or brand like you can.

PR isn't rocket science. Anyone with a great idea, some common sense, and the audacity to try can pitch a story to the media. If you're willing to invest an hour or two a week to research media outlets and contacts you'd like to see your brand appear in, you can work as your own publicist and generate your own media opportunities. In fact, when done right, securing ongoing PR for your brand may become as easy as sending off a few emails or making a few phone calls each week.

As you start applying the lessons learned in this book and undertaking your own PR efforts, I want to warn you that you will come up against rejection—and sometimes ignorance—of your emails, pitches, and phone calls. It's part of the publicity game to hear more nos than yeses in the beginning. While this may leave you frustrated, embarrassed, and annoyed, I encourage you to keep at it. If you are consistent, persistent, and able to learn from your mistakes, you'll be successful at publicity in no time.

CHAPTER TWO
TARGETING YOUR TARGET AUDIENCE

Can I be real with you for one second?

I often hear business owners say they want to get more customers, but their efforts fall flat because they haven't created a solid foundation to attract those fans. Or even to identify who their key customers would be.

That's right, they have no idea who their true target audience is!

Does this also describe you? You shouldn't feel bad. It's incredibly common for a business owner or brand to be clueless about who they truly want to serve as customers.

And no, saying your target audience or ideal customer is everyone is not the right answer.

There's no better time than now to identify your target audience and how you can attract more customers.

In this chapter, I'm going to teach you everything I know about this subject. And, at the risk of sounding like I'm bragging, I'll admit I actually know a thing or two about attracting your target audience.

But first, I need to get real with you. And I apologize in advance if this tough love hurts, but it's for your own good.

Although your brand and offerings might appeal to a large group of people, it doesn't make sense for you to promote them to everyone.

Which is why you need to identify your brand's target audience. Also known as the people who really want or need what you're offering.

IDENTIFYING YOUR TARGETS

How do you identify your target audience?

First, figure out the need for your exact product or service, focusing on what problem it can solve.

Then, refine your target audience by identifying who has bought your product or service in the past.

If your product or service is brand new, a good alternative would be looking at your competitors to get additional insights around who their target audience is and finding where your offering fills in the industry gaps.

The toughest part of this process is you must avoid making assumptions.

For example, say you own a homemade pet biscuit brand. This makes you an expert on the many benefits of homemade pet biscuits and treats. But it would be incorrect for you to assume all consumers know this subject matter and all its nuances as well as you do.

The truth is, they may not even know such a product exists. As tempting as it is to fill in the blanks, you should engage with your potential customers and conduct as much research as possible.

Moving forward, as your business grows, you can continue to evaluate and possibly change your target audience.

For instance, in five years, you may want to expand your product line or even sell internationally.

Or you might think you are catering specifically to men, when in reality you are selling exclusively to wives and girlfriends who are shopping for their fellas.

Knowing which audience you are targeting, and continually refining this group, will ensure you're on the right track with your pitches and what you're promoting.

RESEARCHING AND ANALYZING

How do you identify and analyze your target audience?

First, you need to do your research.

By clearly defining your target audience—whether it's senior citizens, busy moms, or millennials in California— you can easily answer questions and overcome obstacles as you work to promote your brand.

Some of the questions you should ask yourself when trying to identify your target audience include:
- Is the potential audience for your product or service large enough?
- Do you need to alter your PR efforts to best appeal to this audience?
- Should you tailor your messaging in some way to maximize effectiveness?

- How can you target your PR efforts to optimize reach with the most promising potential buyers?

The consumers who find your brand appealing often share similar characteristics, which will help you fine-tune your messaging from top to bottom.

Using this information, you can craft a target audience profile to uncover these shared traits. This includes psychographic data about how your target audience members behave, as well as basic information to help you identify this audience properly.

Here are some demographic criteria to help you get started:
- Age
- Location
- Gender
- Income level
- Education level
- Marital or family status
- Occupation
- Ethnic background

Psychographic criteria goes a little deeper, and can be key in painting a more complete picture of your audience.

Here are some examples of psychographic demographic criteria:
- Interests
- Hobbies
- Values
- Attitudes
- Behaviors
- Lifestyle preferences

Every industry, business, and product is different, so these lists are by no means the end-all-be-all. However, they are an excellent starting point to evaluate the segment size and opportunity surrounding your target audience.

Don't be afraid to make adjustments and include criteria that add interesting layers to your profiles. Remember, the better you know your target audience, the better you can promote your brand to them!

DRILL DOWN DEEPER

As you work through the research on your target audience, try to be as specific as possible. By starting with a detailed audience profile, you'll be able to make the most educated decisions when it comes to crafting compelling PR campaigns.

Entrepreneurs, both new and experienced, often worry that they'll be too specific as they conduct their research, fearing that it will limit their reach.

In reality, identifying a specific target audience helps ensure that you make decisions that are dictated by your true customers, which sets you up for long-term success.

Drill down to who your target audience truly is by zeroing in on their:
- Attitudes
- Beliefs
- Pain points

Understanding their age and income is the first step, but drilling down to the core issues they face are what will help set your brand apart from the competition.

If you do a quick search online, you'll often find existing resources that can help you pull together information about your industry, market segment, competition, and your ideal potential target audience.

The best part of that is someone has already done the work for you!

However, the downside is that the research you find may not be as focused or useful as you'd like it to be.

Below are a few resources to help get you started:
- Quantcast provides free, accurate, and dependable audience insights for over 100 million web and mobile destinations
- Alexa transforms raw data into meaningful insights that will help you find your competitive advantage
- Google Trends uncovers where your target customers are predominantly located

All this information will help you learn more about your target audience so you can develop a strong publicity strategy.

COMPARE AND CONTRAST

While comparison may be the thief of joy, I'd be remiss if I didn't mention taking a look at what your competitors are doing.

Take all you've learned in your research above, and ask yourself these questions about your competitors:
- What's their market positioning?
- What are customers actually purchasing from them?
- What are their customers willing to pay for their offering?
- Would they pay more if you offered something extra?
- What are customers saying on social media?
- What social media channels are they interacting with the most?
- What other interests do they list on their personal social media feeds?
- What do they do for a living?
- What are their hobbies?
- How are they describing their brands or offerings?
- What weaknesses can you identify from their reviews that you may be able to address with your brand?

Depending on how well your competitors are doing, you may want to avoid going after the same exact target audience.

But don't be discouraged!

The purpose of this portion of your research is to identify your competitors' weaknesses and overlooked areas of the market, so that you can capitalize on them to drive success and concentrate promotional efforts around these newly-found opportunities for you.

STRAIGHT TO THE SOURCE

On top of all the research methods we've already addressed, you can learn a lot about your target audience through primary research, which involves gathering data directly from consumers.

Although primary research can be a little more expensive than other methods, it allows you to truly hear the voice of your customer and get answers to specific questions about your brand.

Here are some primary research tools I recommend:
- *Distribute surveys.* Send surveys to existing and potential customers via email or web-based services like Google Forms or SurveyMonkey.
- *Conduct interviews.* Talk to consumers who might fit in your target audience. For example, you could stand in a high-traffic area at a trade show and ask attendees to answer a few short questions.
- *Assemble focus groups.* Get feedback from a small group of consumers who fit your target audience profile using a question and answer sessions or group discussions.

Now that you have some serious insight into who your target audience is, it's time to ask yourself a series questions. Ask yourself:

- Do you feel there are enough potential customers within your target audience to promote your brand?
- Will your target market benefit from your product or service?
- Will this target market see a true need for it? Will they come back repeatedly to purchase?
- Do you understand what drives your target market to make buying decisions?
- Can you reach your market with your key message? How easily accessible are they?

Answering these questions will help you understand if you need to pivot your messaging to appeal to a different target audience, as well as enable you to perform targeted PR efforts that put the right message in front of them continuously.

KEEP IT FRESH

As the marketplace shifts and evolves, your ideal clientele may change. Make sure you stay ahead of the curve, and one step ahead of your competition, by keeping your target audience updated.

To do so, conduct additional primary research and refine your target audience's profile every six to 12 months. This also will help you refine your publicity strategy and brand voice.

PUBLICITY PRACTICE

Are you ready to get out there and identify your target audience using the tips in this chapter?

Start working through the ideas and questions listed in this chapter. And remember, you can always reach out directly to the crowd you feel may be your target audience if you get stuck.

Most importantly, don't forget to dream big and have fun while researching and identifying your target audience or audiences.

CHAPTER THREE
SETTING PR GOALS

Like anything else good in life, there's no better way to achieve all your PR dreams than by being a goal getter.

If you're debating skipping this chapter on goal setting, I ask you to reconsider. The PR goals you dream up here will shape your PR strategy—and ultimately, determine your success with the media.

Why?

Because goals are the means in which we express where our effort is directed. They can be broad, relatively abstract, and even difficult to quantify.

One thing is certain: Goals do matter. Especially as it relates to PR.

By using PR, you aim to create, maintain, and enhance your brand's reputation, position it appropriately in the public eye, and communicate messages about it through traditional and social media.

When you share the story of your brand in a way that makes the media sit up and take notice, that's PR, and it does things like build awareness of your brand and raise your profile publicly.

These goals are all very important for a business but, again, can be hard to measure.

Will PR produce income for your business tomorrow? Probably not. But, PR does generate and build audiences. Using sales and marketing techniques will then turn those audiences into sales leads.

This means you need metrics outside of sales to measure the return on investment you're getting from your PR efforts.

Gauging the overall effectiveness of your PR efforts requires examining how well you're reaching your target audience and how that's affecting your customers and prospects. Before you get started on any promotional tactics or media pitching.

Here are some suggestions for setting PR goals for your brand and measuring their success.

ASK YOURSELF WHY

First, answer the question "why?"

Before you start a publicity campaign or even send one pitch to the media, ask yourself: "Why am I investing the time or money to do this? What do I want to get out of it?"

Once you know those answers, you can better direct your PR efforts.

You wouldn't put together a plan for remodeling your kitchen without knowing the desired result, would you? The same holds true for PR.

Don't put together a plan without knowing the desired results and don't confuse these desired results with strategies.

For example, getting articles about your brand in the media, isn't the goal of your PR efforts. It's a part of your overall publicity strategy.

Rather, your goal in this instance might be to increase the number of prospect email addresses you collect through your website or to create more positive public sentiment and awareness toward your brand.

DEFINE WHAT'S VALUABLE

The second thing to take into account when setting PR goals, is to define what is valuable.

Because PR isn't marketing, you can't necessarily measure return on investment in terms of sales.

In fact, various business studies have shown that PR often represents just five to seven percent of sales.

Try defining what is valuable to your brand—the ROI may not necessarily be a bottom line outcome.

It may be you're looking for repeat visits to your website, a change in the perception of your brand, or a shift how your customers interact with your brand.

And if you do experience a bump in sales that occurs whenever you have a PR campaign running, that becomes another way to quantify the success of your efforts.

MEASURE YOUR COVERAGE

Measuring your media coverage also is crucial to setting your PR goals.

Media coverage is a big part of PR, so look at where your brand is getting coverage or take into account where you want your brand to be securing more.

Are these publications, podcasts, TV shows, and other media outlets reaching the specific targets that are important to your brand?

You'll want to make note and adjust your PR efforts accordingly.

KEEP YOUR CUSTOMERS SATISFIED

While setting PR goals, you also want to look at customer retention and satisfaction.

If you have a publicity strategy in place that aims to improve the perception of your brand—whether that's quality, trust, fashionableness, or something similar—you can measure it by surveying customers before your PR efforts begin and after they end.

Keeping your customers satisfied, and as customers, is key to running a successful business. Make sure you don't overlook them when determining your PR goals.

POSITION YOUR BRAND PROPERLY

You also will want to look at how you and your brand are being positioned when setting your PR goals.

Are you—and the brand—being positioned as an expert and leader in your industry? Are members of the media seeking you out for your expert advice? What is the public perception of your brand currently?

The answers to these questions matter.

BE ANALYTICAL

Just as with social media and marketing, analytics matter in PR. Use them to your advantage.

Analytics are a key part of discovering how your PR efforts will impact the awareness, attitudes, and behavior of your audience.

Although you want to look at impressions and mentions, you also want to watch where your clicks are coming from. You also will want to take note of things like increases in newsletter subscriptions, the number of calls you're receiving, visits to your website, or in-person visits to your store.

You know why surveys always ask you how you heard about a company? It's the easiest way to track word of mouth and promotional efforts!

Don't overlook your opportunity to use analytics like these to your advantage.

BE PRO SEO

Finally, measure your SEO performance.

As you work through your PR activities, look at increases or decreases in branded search terms in Google Tools and see how many visits to your website result from those searches.

Determine if social media followings increase during your PR efforts or after media coverage.

You can also compare conversion and bounce rates for traffic that comes from publications that have covered your brand, to determine which ones will be the best to target in future PR efforts. As well as who you can leave off your PR outreach list in the future.

WHY PR GOALS MATTER

By carefully assessing the outcomes of your PR endeavors against your original PR goals, you'll be able to make more informed decisions about how you spend your future PR dollars and time. Which means you'll be able to know exactly how to get the most bang for your buck.

Pretty amazing, huh?

PR GOALS IN ACTION

We've covered a lot of ground in this chapter already, but I want to make sure I'm giving you a concrete example of how this information can be applied in the real world.

Say you're about to open a store in your town. Your PR goals might be the following:

1. *Promote goodwill.* One of the most straight-forward PR goals is to enhance your brand's goodwill. Goodwill means a generally positive rapport with the communities in which you do business.

    Having this strong connection helps drive customers to your business and also aids in building long-term loyal relationships with key customers. Getting involved in community activities and participating in charitable programs are common techniques to promote goodwill with the community.

2. *Raise awareness.* Another common PR goal is to raise awareness of your brand and offerings. This can coincide with advertising campaigns with similar objectives. Raising awareness is an important step for new brands or businesses that have not yet established strong recognition in the marketplace. Media articles, featured mentions or stories, and participation in industry events can all help boost the recognition of a brand.

3. *Change attitudes.* Often PR efforts have the purpose of improving or reshaping the general public's attitude about your brand.

   Companies that struggle with negative perceptions in the market often use PR to promote a message of community involvement, charitable giving, or product benefits for the common good.

   Companies on the grow can work to change attitudes when they want to take their target customer's general perception and turn it on its head.

4. *Informing and educating.* Many PR efforts have a direct goal of informing certain audiences. For instance, your new store may send out weekly email newsletters to offer free advice on how your products tie into the season's latest trends. The hope is that regularly staying in front of customers with messages that are useful will help your brand maintain top-of-mind awareness. Plus, providing free and useful information can generate positive sentiments from the market.

PUBLICITY PRACTICE

Now it's your turn to take action and apply the tips in this chapter to your brand.

Spend some time thinking over what truly matters for you and your brand as it relates to PR. Then, take action by asking yourself the questions in this chapter and getting to work.

Don't worry about knowing all the answers or getting it perfect the first time. The key is for you to start brainstorming and getting your ideas down on paper.

CHAPTER FOUR
BRAINSTORMING BRAND WORDS

For more than two decades, I've encouraged entrepreneurs and influencers to find words that describe their brand perfectly.

I'd explain how important the words they chose were, how they should use their words, and even how to integrate them into their customer's entire experience.

But here's the kicker: I never fully explained how entrepreneurs and influencers should go about finding these words by themselves.

Which I now realize is like telling someone to make my favorite dessert without telling them exactly what that treat is.

Finding the right words is hard. But nothing worth having comes easily, right?

In this chapter, we'll work through how to make finding the right words for your brand happen.

DEFINING BRAND WORDS

There's a reason why out of all the PR tactics in the world, I chose to put the chapter about key messages and brand words near the front.

Why? Because key messages and brand words are such personal things.

You are the driving force behind your brand. And you are the one who ultimately decides which ones to put out into the world to describe your brand.

And, while I am many things, I am not the be all, end all critic on what is proper English or writing.

I'm definitely not going to be offering technical tips for writing in this action plan. But I do want to help you capture the vision behind your brand and extend that into all the promotional activities you put out into the world.

That's what we'll be focusing on in this chapter, how to write key messages that clearly communicate your brand.

We also will discuss how to choose the right brand words so your messaging is always on point—no matter what you're pitching and promoting through publicity.

Let's dive on in, starting with brand words.

Your brand words are the three or four words you want people to think, feel, or say about your brand.

For example, for my dress company vieve and jo, my brand words are effortless, glamorous, cheerful, and classic.

How did I arrive at these four words that fit my brand? Let's walk you through the process.

Because, let's be real, finding the right words to describe your brand—which is in essence, your baby—is hard.

Your brand words are a reflection of you—not just your business.

When someone visits your website or reads your blog, they are having a conversation with you. They aren't just simply reading words on a screen.

That is why it's so important to determine how you speak to them.

CHOOSING YOUR WORDS

When choosing your brand words, you first need to look at who you are attracting.

More than anything, it's important to understand the type of audience your brand attracts. They're clearly visiting your site or social media feeds for a reason. But you need to know why.

What do they want that you can provide?

Are they trying to style their hair a certain way and you can offer a tutorial?

Are they searching for a low-carb recipe and you offer the tastiest option?

Are they struggling to keep their Fiddle Fig plant alive and you know the secret trick?

Ask yourself why and list the reasons.

It is equally important to understand how your audience feels just before they visit your site or social media. This means you need to get real and tap into their emotional state so you can write captions and content that pertains to their needs and struggle.

For instance, if someone has recently gained weight, he or she is probably embarrassed, perhaps sad, and definitely overwhelmed by all the choices out there.

Tap into that!

If someone is looking for the perfect bag in the shade of cobalt blue, she is looking to shop and ready to learn what else she can accessorize with it.

Speak to her in her language so she buys from you!

Ask yourself what questions your target audience is asking themselves before they visit you and how you can answer them.

Next, get real about the experiences you want others to associate with your brand.

When someone sees your logo or brand name, what do you want them to feel?

Is your brand fun, wild, safe, modern?

Now ask yourself why.

Why is your brand fun? Why is it wild?

What does that mean to your audience and how will it affect their experience with your brand?

Remember, the energy you put out into the world is the energy you receive back from it.

If your brand words are raw, edgy, and push social norms, be ready to receive the exact same back from the audience you attract.

At the end of the day, your brand is a reflection of the service you provide and of you as a person.

Be mindful of that.

Finally, it's important to know how you want your target audience to feel.

We've already discussed figuring out how your targets felt just before turning to your brand. For this portion of the exercise, let's change gears.

How do you want your target audience to feel after they visit your site or interact with your brand?

Do you want to leave them feeling hopeful? Inspired? Excited? Invincible?

WORDS IN ACTION

The key here is to understand how your customers' emotions relate to the offerings you provide.

If you want them to feel a certain way after they touch your brand, you must speak to them in a way that communicates these emotions.

Let's use a dress line as an example.

Who is the dress line attracting? It's attracting busy females in their 30s and beyond who want to look glamorous without a ton of effort.

They are passionate about their individual style, yet still want to be comfortable. And with that comfort, comes confidence.

Notice the words I reused? Glamorous, comfortable.

What experiences do I want associated with the dress line's brand? Confidence and beauty comes from being comfortable, as well as comfortable with who you are.

Being put together shouldn't take a ton of effort, it should be effortless. And if you're going to stand out, you might as well be the brightest, most cheerful one in the room.

Again, take note of the words I'm using: confidence, comfortable, cheerful, effortless.

Now how do I want my dress line's target audience to feel? That they don't have to sacrifice glamour for comfort. Or individual style in order to wear a classic silhouette.

Each of this dress line's customers are unique and bold and can be effortlessly glamorous in a brightly-colored dress, while still being comfortable.

Are you hearing more repetition in my word choices?

Figuring out your brand words can be this simple!

When the time comes to write a blog post, use your voice on social media, or write your key messages, be sure to use your brand words.

Remember, your brand is what sets you apart from your competition, so chose the words you use to represent it wisely.

Which is an excellent lead-in to our next chapter and the most important messages you'll ever craft for your brand—your key messages.

PUBLICITY PRACTICE

Now it's your turn to take action and apply the tips in this chapter to your brand.

Spend some time thinking over what sets you apart from your competition. Then, brainstorm words you can use to represent your brand.

Don't worry about getting your brand words perfect on your first try. The key is for you to brainstorm words, get a feel for them as they apply to your brand, and see how your customers and potential customers relate to your word choices.

CHAPTER FIVE
KICKASS KEY MESSAGES

In the age of social media, it's important to remember that it isn't just pretty pictures posted on feeds that are all that's needed to sell your brand.

Here's what truly matters: Defining your voice by understanding what you're really saying and how you want your target audience to feel. Words matter—especially when it comes to your brand.

Do you want your brand to be perceived in a certain way?

Do you want your customers to remember you or your brand a certain way?

Do you want your customers to describe you or your brand a certain way?

Then you need key messages.

Not to be overly dramatic, but key messages are the most important and impactful words that tell your brand's story.

It's true. Keep reading and I'll tell you why.

DEFINING KEY MESSAGES

By definition, key messages are the most important and impactful words that will tell your brand's story.

They are the main points you want your target audience to hear and remember.

Key messages are the main takeaways that you want anyone who comes into contact with your brand to quickly understand.

They create meaning and headline the issues you want to discuss.

Key messages also allow you to control communications, enhance relationships with your target audiences, and are an important feature of any publicity strategy.

And, key messages bring your brand words and all your marketing collateral together in three or four succinct and easily memorable sentences.

CREATING KEY MESSAGES

To ensure you get your point across, it's essential to establish your key messages before any outreach to the media or performing any PR tactics aimed at your target audience.

When creating your key messages, use these steps as your guide:

1. *Ask these questions.* Is my key message believable and supported by evidence? Is it easy to understand, concise, and professional? Is my key message positive? Is it purposeful? Does my key message represents my agenda appropriately?
2. *Keep it simple.* Your key messages should be short and specific. Make sure you work out the most important thoughts you wish to portray and write simply but with enough interest to provoke your reader.
3. *Target your messages.* Consider your target audiences when drafting your key messages. What do they need and want to hear from you? Do you have multiple audiences? If so, tailor your key messages to each group.
4. *Control your communication.* Quite often, what we say is not always interpreted or heard by the receiver in the same way we originally meant it to be. Influencing the perceptions of other people is not an easy task. But, by developing key messages that are clear, concise, truthful, and positive, you will put yourself in control of the information that is out there. You also will allow yourself to influence your audience in the most effective way.
5. *Revew and refresh.* Key messages are meant to be fluid, not static. Everything changes over time, so reviewing your key messages every six to eight months is vital in making sure they are still relevant and reflect your brand.

If your key messages address these five steps, your key messages are good to go. And it won't be long before the audience you're seeking to become customers start buying from you or looking to you as the expert in your field.

KEY MESSAGE TIPS

If you're still stuck on drafting your key messages, take a deep breath.

While important, key messages aren't monumental sentences that will sink your brand's ship. They should be words and phrases you use—or have heard your top customers use—to describe you or your brand in daily interactions.

In order to be effective, key messages also should be:
- *Few in number.* Think no more than three or four sentences.
- *Concise.* Key messages should be delivered in seven seconds or less.
- *Free of any jargon.* Select messages even your Grandmother can understand.
- *Relevant.* Your message has to make sense and pass the sniff test.
- *Consistent.* A good key message allows the essence of your brand to always remain.
- *Repeatable.* Key messages should be easy to remember and repeat.

KEY MESSAGES IN ACTION

While they will change and shift over time, as your brand does, key messages should firmly state what you want customers and potential customers to now about your brand.

For example, key messages for my dress line, vieve and jo, could be:
1. vieve and jo is a line of effortlessly glamourous dresses in vibrant colors.
2. We make beautiful dresses for every body.
3. We think being comfortable is empowering to women, starting with how they dress.
4. We believe brights are the new black, because life is too short to wear neutrals.

All four sentences are short. They're sweet. Easy to remember. And they feature the brand's key words throughout.

UPDATING YOUR KEY MESSAGES

Although key messages support your mission, values, and brand at the outset, you should ensure they still meet your and audience needs over time.

For many, January is often the ideal time for a key message review and refresh for most brands. While for others, they plan to revisit their key messages as the seasons change.

Truth is, there is no right or wrong time to update your key messages. I recommend putting a reminder into your calendar to check your key messages from time to time to ensure they are still relevant and accurate.

I hope you'll use this chapter and the accompanying publicity practice section to create a foundation that communicates exactly what your brand is about.

PUBLICITY PRACTICE

Now it's your turn to take action and apply the tips in this chapter to your brand.

Spend some time brainstorming the most important and impactful messages that will help tell your brand's story in the best way to your target audience.

Ask yourself:
- What do you want your target audience to hear and remember?
- What are the main takeaways that you want anyone who comes into contact with your brand to quickly understand?

- What headlines do you want shared about your brand?

Remember, your key messages are going to be fluid. What works now may not be a fit for your brand next year. What matters is that you identify key messages that speak to your brand story and your target audience.

CHAPTER SIX
ELEVATING YOUR ELEVATOR SPEECH

Let's chat about the first time I was left alone in a business setting as an adult to network and share my elevator speech.

Not only was the idea of interacting with complete strangers daunting, the idea of trying to pique their interest left me downright queasy.

Like, clean up on aisle seven queasy.

I can still remember what it felt like to stand alone in that room, with my palms sweating, my heart racing, and my throat closing. I wanted to disappear.

But I didn't.

Today, I find myself interacting nonstop with strangers, jumping on cold calls, and ready to break the ice in any room.

Sure, I still get nervous. But having an elevator speech I can depend on has revolutionized my business (and life).

I hope you'll find the information included in this chapter helpful as you strengthen your approach to publicity.

WHY ELEVATOR SPEECHES MATTER

If you had less than one minute to explain to a stranger who you are, what you do, and how you can educate, help, inform, or entertain them, what would you say?

Furthermore, could you do it in two sentences or less?

Well, that's exactly what your target audience wants you to do.

In fact, according to the leading science journals, the human attention span is now less than that of a goldfish. Which is less than six seconds

That's not a ton of time!

What this means, is that you better use every second you can to attract your target audience's attention and make sure they not only take note of your brand, but also know what's in it for them by purchasing from you.

In this chapter, I'll walk you through exactly how you can create an elevator speech that has your target audience lining up to hear more from you.

WHAT IS AN ELEVATOR SPEECH

Before you can have the world's greatest elevator speech, you first need to know what one is.

By definition, an elevator speech is a brief summary or pitch relating to your brand, that can be made in about 30 seconds. Or roughly, the time it takes one to ride in the typical elevator and tell someone their abbreviated life story.

As a rule of thumb, I always like to aim for 100 words or less for my elevator speeches. This way, when you need to submit a super-short, 100 word or less bio for a speaking gig, award entry, or media opportunity, you've already got yours nailed down and ready to go.

WHY ELEVATOR SPEECHES MATTER

Why is an elevator speech so important?

Because you only get one chance to make a first impression.

An elevator speech can help you make the most of these first impressions while making pitching and networking situations easier and more productive.

An elevator speech also helps in situations where you might be uncomfortable or get a little tongue tied when trying to explain what you do. It gives you a ready-to-go introduction, which can take a lot of the stress out of any situation.

Plus, having a well-practiced elevator speech will present you as more confident and self-assured leading to a great first impression.

WHAT TO PUT IN YOURS

What should you say in your elevator speech?

The point of creating an elevator speech is to design a statement that explains to someone with limited knowledge of your brand or industry, what you do, how you do it, and who you do it for.

Your elevator speech should be simple, concise, and easy to understand.

The key is you want your audience to remember you, yet you don't want to make them have to think too hard while you're giving them your elevator speech.

Remember your brand words and key messages? This is where they come into play.

By using your brand words and key messages together in unison, you form the perfect harmony that is an elevator speech.

All while sharing the exact messages you want to leave your audience with.

ONLY THE ESSENTIALS

What are the essential elements of an elevator speech?

Above all else, your elevator speech needs to be goal orientated and targeted.

Ask yourself, what is the reason behind my brand and who am I talking to?

Or, why would the person I'm speaking to be interested in my brand?

You may need to create a different elevator speech depending on your different objectives and audiences. Which can easily be done by tweaking a few words here or there.

Try to include a hook. This is the element that captures your listener's attention and makes them want to know more.

Also, try to use words or phrases that strike a chord in your listener.

Again this is a perfect time to use the the brand words and key messages that we discussed in a previous issue.

SIX EASY STEPS

I know what you're thinking, "This is all great, KJ, but where do I even start with writing my elevator speech?"

Don't worry, friend, I've got you!

First, write down what you do.

Get a pen and paper out and write or type out on your laptop what you do in different ways at least 10 times.

This is only the first step. Don't be too particular about what you're writing, just generate ideas and get a feel for descriptive words.

Second, determine your objective.

What is the point of your elevator speech?

Do you want to gain a new customer, make a sale, enlist support for an idea, or entice the media to write about you?

Third, develop action statements.

Create 10-12 statements or questions designed to act as a call to action in association with your objective.

Next, record yourself.

Sure, it sounds silly; however, listening to a recording of yourself, while daunting, can help you be more critical of your word choices and help you narrow down your approach.

Post-recording, get a second opinion.

While I'm not a huge fan of entertaining the peanut gallery, in this instance I support outside opinions.

Once you have made necessary edits and perfected your elevator speech to fit into a 30 second time frame, run it by as many people as you can. This will help you practice with people you trust that already have some understanding of what it is you do. I've found that colleagues, customers, friends, and family often provide the best feedback.

Now you have your final elevator speech. Guess what that means?

Yep, you guessed it. It's time to practice, practice, practice!

PRACTICE MAKES PERFECT

As you start to practice your elevator speech more and more, you'll get to a point where it starts to feel perfect.

Write it down and make sure you memorize it so that you are comfortable delivering it in any situation.

Last but not least, continue to practice and perfect your elevator speech. Sure, it maybe be perfect now; however, there is always room for improvement.

Listen for phrases that could help make your elevator speech more clear, concise, or powerful.

Are the words you're using the ones that will attract your true target customer? Be honest.

As you, your brand, your goals, your customers, and your business change, you will need to adapt your elevator speech accordingly to reflect these changes.

CRAFTING YOUR ELEVATOR SPEECH

Think you're ready to craft your elevator speech?

Here are some tips to keep in mind as you do:
1. *Know your brand.* What are the key offerings of your brand? Who are your customers? Remember to include only the most important takeaways that you want a potential new customer or business partner to hear. Keep it succinct.
2. *Be adaptable.* Understand to whom you're speaking and adapt your elevator speech to fit his or her needs. If you're speaking to a potential customer in the consumer space, position your information accordingly. If you're speaking to a member of the media, make sure you hit on relevant pieces of information they would want to include in a feature on your brand. In both cases, be ready for multiple questions or reactions.
3. *Have a hook.* Just like a media pitch, the first sentence of your elevator speech should grab the listener's attention right away. Give her or him a reason to listen to you. Don't bore your audience to tears, or worse, have them tune you out before you even get started talking.
4. *End with a call to action.* Close your elevator speech with explicit directions for a next step. Whether that is visiting your website, directing interested parties to your social feeds, or closing a sale, make sure your listener knows where to go or what to expect next.

It really is that easy!

FOOL-PROOF FORMULA

A fool-proof formula for a killer elevator speech could be something like:

Who (you are) for (target audience or customer). What (they need or want). Your brand/product/service provides (key benefit, compelling reason to buy). And how they can reach you (or make a purchase).

Want to see this formula in action? Here's an example, using my vieve and jo dress line:

vieve and jo is a line of effortlessly glamorous dresses in vibrant colors. As a brand, we believe being comfortable is empowering to women and that life is too short to wear neutrals. Our designs encourage women like you to shine brightly and boldly.

You'd be intrigued hearing that, right?

ENERGIZE YOUR ELEVATOR

Repeat after me: No one likes a boring elevator speech.

Whether you're trying to gain the interest of a potential customer, get the attention of the media, or simply explain what you do, having a strong elevator speech is your key to success.

Have fun with it!

Throw in your brand words—and some color. And by color, I mean it's totally acceptable to use colorful language.

Make sure your key messages are represented, as well as your brand words, your voice, and your personality.

Look, just like no one wants to be sold to constantly—no one likes a boring elevator speech.

What's memorable about something that's boring? Nothing!

So don't be that person.

DIGGING DOWN DEEP

While a lot of the information in this chapter is geared towards in-person networking and focusing on perfecting how you'd verbally give your elevator speech, the same principles listed within this guide apply across a wide variety of mediums.

For instance, once you can succinctly deliver your elevator speech in 100 words or less, challenge yourself to deliver it in 150 characters or less as your bio on social media.

Then, take it one step farther and start using your elevator speech as a single sentence in your email pitches to the media.

Remember, your elevator speech is basically your bio (or your brand's bio) said clearly and concisely like a verbal (or written) business card.

You want to get your key messages and brand words out there in a way that informs and catches the attention of whomever you are speaking with. Because, even if they may not be your ideal target audience, they may have a friend, sibling, colleague, child, or partner who may just be.

A killer elevator speech not only sets you up for future success with customers and the media, it also makes sure you're telling your story, your way.

PUBLICITY PRACTICE

Now it's your turn to take action and apply the tips in this chapter to your brand.

Spend some time thinking over what you'd like to say in your elevator speech. Then, take action by getting to work and writing it down and rehearsing.

Don't worry if the answers don't come to you immediately. The key is for you to start brainstorming and getting your ideas down on paper.

CHAPTER SEVEN
MAKING YOUR MEDIA LIST

Say you have the perfect PR pitch ready to go and the only thing standing between you and total media domination was sending it to the appropriate media contact.

Would you know exactly which media contact to send your pitch to?

Furthermore, would you have the appropriate contact information to get your pitch in that media contact's hands?

This is the exact reason why you need a media list.

Lucky for you, in this chapter I'll walk you through exactly how you can create a standout media list and how you can identify the appropriate media contacts to populate it with.

WHAT IS A MEDIA LIST

Not sure what a media list even is? No worries, friend!

In a nutshell, a media list documents the key contacts—media or otherwise—who would be interested in receiving information about you or your brand.

These media contacts may include marketing executives, reporters, bloggers, producers, freelance writers, and editors across print, online, blogs, radio, and television.

The process of building a media list allows you to think long and hard about who will be receiving your news and how you might approach each journalist, blogger, producer, or editor to ensure they see value in covering your story.

For this reason, it's important to selectively target the media of most relevance to your brand.

To build your brands' thought leadership and demonstrate expertise in your industry, you must be strategic about where you generate your media coverage.

WHO TO INCLUDE

Here are some tips to help create an excellent media list.

The first thing you need to decide when creating your media list is who your target audience is and how best to reach them.

Remember when we talked about researching your target audience in a previous chapter? If you haven't already gathered this information during your initial target audience research, start by researching what your target audience is interested in and how they prefer to consume information, including via blogs, websites, TV programs, newspapers, or magazines.

For instance, if your target audience is predominately busy moms, you would look at directly targeting your media pitches to women's magazines and mom blogs.

If we revisit my dress line that we've discussed in earlier chapters, which has the target audience of women over the age of 30, we would look at directly targeting our media pitches to women's magazines, as well as lifestyle blogs and digital outlets.

It's important to conduct research into relevant media outlets. This should include what topics they cover, the medium (like is the outlet online, a radio station or show, a television station or show, and so on) plus the outlet's readership or audience size.

It also is important to take note of the frequency the media outlets publish or produce new content. For instance, a blog may publish posts daily but a magazine will often be published monthly.

Understanding the editorial calendar and the deadlines of each media outlet you're targeting will give your pitch the best chance of landing.

When creating a media list, it also is important to find the best person to contact at each media outlet. This person should have responsibility for or an interest in the topic of your industry or brand.

For example, if you are looking to send a media pitch to the technology section of a metropolitan newspaper, you would need to find the journalist who covers that particular section.

If you are looking to send a pitch about dresses to a media contact at a national women's magazine, you should look for the specific fashion editor that covers that niche.

Look at articles written about your area of expertise in your target media outlets and note the media contacts who wrote these articles.

This also an excellent time to perform a competitive analysis and research which media outlets your competitors have appeared in. You can easily find this information using Google to search or by visiting the press pages on their websites. List out the media outlets they have been featured in. Use this as the start of your media list.

It is also helpful to look at the job titles of journalists, producers and reporters. Often their particular area of expertise will be reflected in their job title. For instance, sports reporter or beauty editor.

MEDIA LIST TIPS

When pulling together your media list, make note of these tried and true PR tips.

Try to avoid sending your pitches to the email address for general inquiries or the news desk, as often it will not reach the right person at the media outlet.

Ensure you don't contact several people at the same media outlet with the exact same pitch, as they may feel that you are spamming them. To find media contact details, you can visit the media outlet's website where they may list staff email addresses and phone numbers, or call the publication directly for information.

You also can do something that today may seem unheard of— you can physically go and visit a bookstore or newsstand and immense yourself in the magazine aisles. Once there, you can research the different kinds of articles being written about your industry, and by whom. The front of each publication not only holds the magazine's table of contents, but also holds valuable names, email addresses, and other contact information for staffers at that publication.

As you cannot verify it beforehand and since media contacts frequently move around, I never recommend purchasing a media list from an unknown source. For the same fee, you can easily invest time yourself—or by hiring an intern or virtual assistant—to help pull together a media list on your behalf.

FOOL-PROOF FORMAT

Once you start compiling your list, it is important to organize your media list in a database, such as an Excel document, with separate columns for the name of the media outlet, contact person, job title, email address, and phone number.

It is also a good idea to categorize your media list into different sections for the type of media outlet. For example, you can create a section for your blogging contacts and a separate section for your magazine contacts.

Making sure your information is well organized will mean you are able to easily digest the information and locate it quickly.

KEEPING IT FRESH

It is equally important to update your media list regularly, as your media contacts will often change roles or move into a different area of expertise.

To stay updated on who is where, read industry news so you can keep an eye out for changes. This also is helpful so you know when media outlets are launching, shifting their focus, or ceasing publication. And will make sure you're the first to know when new editors or producers have been appointed.

Staying on top of changes within media outlets will ensure that your media list stays up-to-date.

PUBLICITY PRACTICE

Having a great media list is an important start when looking to engage with the media and gain media coverage for your business.

Now it's time to make that list and check it twice! Use the tips in this chapter to help share your brand's story with the media.

Remember, your media list is going to be fluid. Which reporter is working where will change over time. What matters is that you identify at least 15 media contacts to start pitching your brand to and get started.

CHAPTER EIGHT
CREATING CONTENT CALENDARS

I know they say that one should never pick their favorite child, but I must admit, I'm really excited about diving into this chapter and it just may be my favorite.

Why?

Because next to watching an entrepreneur's face light up when they receive the media recognition they've been dreaming about, brainstorming ideas and populating content calendars with story ideas is my favorite thing about PR.

I know I've mentioned it before, but you are the driving force behind your brand. Only you can share your expertise in your own unique way and position your brand as you see it.

And, not to be that person—but just being honest—I'm really ridiculously good at identifying new and unique ways to cover the same story or industry trend.

I live for it.

And in this chapter, I want to teach you the exact step-by-step process I follow when laying out a successful 12-month brand-specific content calendar.

Yes, that's exactly what we'll be focusing on in these pages, how to populate a content calendar and clearly communicate all the different facets of your brand.

We also will discuss how to choose the right marketing holidays and seasonal happenings so your pitches are always on point—no matter what your industry.

Let's get started, shall we?

WHAT IS A CONTENT CALENDAR

Before I get too far ahead of myself, I want to make sure we're on the same page as far as what a content calendar, also known as a PR promo calendar, editorial calendar, or pitch calendar, truly is.

A content calendar is a 12-month calendar of content that shows you what to pitch (and when) so that you can share the appropriate info with your target audience as well as the media.

All on a consistent basis.

I know what you're thinking: "But KJ, I already have to develop new products, plan out my social media posts, keep up with shipping, and market my services. Why do I need a content calendar?"

Funny you should ask.

In my more than two decades in PR working with clients, they tend to have one of two problems with promotions and publicity.

Either, they can't think of anything to promote. Or, they have so much going on, that they're overwhelmed—which means they are firing off content left and right and overwhelming their audiences.

Both cause huge problems. Which lead to inactivity. Meaning nothing gets promoted. In turn, this leads to no revenue.

Can you see why this is a problem?

Enter in the solution: A content calendar!

WHY YOU NEED A CONTENT CALENDAR

Outside of the reasons listed above, here are three key reasons why you need a content calendar.

Above all else, a content calendar helps you maintain consistency with your messages. Consistency is crucial when it comes to publicizing and promoting your brand.

Once you've set expectations with your target audience, you must maintain them.

If you hire influencers to all post on one day to promote your newest product, and then don't ever have them mention it again, it's a waste. Of everyone's time and potentially your promotional budget. Especially if you yourself haven't been mentioning or promoting your latest offering.

That's where a content calendar comes in.

A content calendar will help you strategically plan when and where to promote your messages, products, brand, and collaborations. It can even help you see when you have more content to use than usual. Which allows you the flexibility to post more or push that content to another week.

On the reverse side, a content calendar also alerts you to when your content is light. Allowing you advanced notice to gather new material or brainstorm more pitch ideas with time to spare.

A content calendar isn't just for planning your future content, it also can be used to record what you've previously promoted.

Think about it, you have a lot going on. Yes, you!

It isn't always easy keeping track of how often you've mentioned your latest freebie or when your next sale is happening.

How do you know what you want to promote this February isn't the exact same thing you promoted last February?

Or, what if last February was your greatest month in sales? Don't you want to know what you were pitching and promoting to have been so successful?

For this reason, you can use your content calendar as system of record. And you'll never be in the dark again.

By maintaining a content calendar, you help yourself stay on track with your key messages.

As a rule of thumb, I operate by the 3GT Rule—a rule which says I will post three educational and entertaining posts (I call these gives) for every one promotional post (I call these takes).

Get it, 3GT Rule: three gives, one take?

I use this approach across all my publicity channels—in email marketing, on my blogs, and especially on social media.

This strategy allows me to find common ground with my target audiences. It also allows me to get to know them and gain their trust. Which, in turn, provides common ground for them to one day purchase my products, services, or other offerings.

Using a content calendar is a key part in keeping my PR and publicity efforts balanced, as it allows me to see the big picture on what types of promotions I'm sharing and when.

CONTENT CALENDAR PROCESS

Want to learn the exact process I use when creating my content calendar? Well, you're in luck because I'm about to share it with you.

First, get out a calendar.

Now, you can get all fancy, schmancy with your Apple or Android technology; however, I like to hoof it to Office Depot and purchase a blank desk calendar.

You know, the one where you still have to write in the month and each day in the blank squares.

Those are my jam!

Then, pick the month you wish to start your content calendar in.

Get ready, because you're about to map out 12 months of pitches and promotions for your business.

Next, it's time to identify your holidays.

Go through the next 12 months on your calendar, and pencil in all the relevant holidays.

Make sure you include both marketing holidays and the actual national holidays. Select only those that apply (even if loosely) to your target audience or brand.

Using my dress line example from previous chapters, I definitely will include Easter, any holidays where parties are prevalent, as well as marketing holidays that appeal to women ages 30-plus in the mix. I probably won't include holidays that skew towards males or don't align with the values of my brand.

The next thing you'll want to do is lay out the seasonal opportunities in your content calendar.

Going month-by-month, mark down the seasonal topics that apply to your brand for each point in time.

Again, using my dress line as an example, you might use:
- January: Fresh starts and new looks
- March: Spring trends
- May: What's hot to wear this summer
- August: Back-to-school and fall trends
- November/December: Gift guides and holiday party trends

As you work your way through the months, you're going to quickly see how full a calendar can get.

This is a good thing!

Now that your content calendar is starting to fill up, it's important to go back and revisit your overall PR goal or goals.

After making sure everything you've added to date is in line with your PR goals, it's time to identify where your sales or promotions fit in your content calendar.

Obviously, holiday promotions are huge. Make sure you allocate the appropriate time and planning for these.

Again, using my dress line as an example, I would focus on spring trends, wedding season, Valentine's Day, and similar points in time as ones to pay special attention to. I also would place the majority of my pitches and incorporate promotions around these same points in time.

From another perspective, if you are a brand that serves busy moms, you may instead want to focus on the first of the year, end of school, summer vacations, back to school, and the holidays are your pitch- and promotion-heavy times. For all of these, you can easily pitch how your brand can make a busy mom's life easier.

Because money makes the world go round, I would be remiss if I didn't remind you to put important sales and other related events on your content calendar.

Yes, seasonal and annual sales should be included on your content calendar!

Did you really think Nordstroms wasn't performing a full-blown PR and influencer campaign around their semi-annual sale?

Of course they are, friend!

Follow their lead and make sure you put your sales on your content calendar.

Laying out these important dates on your calendar can help you to not only plan for what is to come, but also to determine when your quiet months may occur.

Then you can plan accordingly.

Now it's time to get really creative. Up until this point, we've been building the skeleton of your content calendar. It's time now to look your calendar over and start filling in the gaps.

Start planning what content you need to create—pitches, promotions, or otherwise—each week to make it happen.

This can include social media posts, additional in-store or online promotions, blog content, special events, media pitches, and more.

KEEP IT FRESH

I want to remind you that nothing on your content calendar has to be set in stone.

It all can be altered and moved around. You know, leave room for a little creativity, would you?

Plus, there are times when what you first planned out in January of one year may no longer hold true by October of that same year.

And that's okay!

Just make sure your changes, additions, and edits all tie back into your PR goals.

WHERE TO START

Not sure where to start when creating your content calendar?

Ask yourself these questions:
- What are the recent trends in my industry?

- What gaps in my industry does my brand fill that my competitors do not?
- Who is perfect for what I offer?
- What questions am I asked all the time?

You can theme 12 months of your content—that's one entire year—by writing down the top 12 questions you're asked all the time by customers, your target audience, friends, or family.

REAL TALK

We've spent so much time together while you've been reading this book, that I consider us the best of friends at this point. Which is why I want to be really real with you, friend.

THIS PART IS HARD.

Don't rush through creating your content calendar. Take your time.

This final step will involve a lot of reading past emails and scraps of paper, but it will produce tons of pitchable ideas.

And then you'll have a solid, media-friendly content calendar just screaming to be pitched and promoted.

PUBLICITY PRACTICE

Now that you've worked through all the ways to populate a content calendar, how to identify which seasonal holidays and marketing holidays are right for your brand, the time-sensitive happenings you want your target audience to associate with your brand, and when you should be pitching and promoting what, it's time to take action!

Trust me, there is no better feeling in the world than having the next 12 months of your content planned out for your brand. It saves so much time!

But, full disclosure, working through the tips outlined in this chapter will take a bit more time. And that's more than okay.

Even if you only start by planning the first or first few months, the goal is to start putting together the pieces so you can have a solid publicity strategy that attracts your target audience and helps you achieve your PR goals.

CHAPTER NINE
MEDIA PITCHING PERFECTION

According to Albert Einstein, if you can't explain it simply, you don't understand it well enough.

I'm pretty sure good, old Al wasn't exactly talking about pitching the media, but he may as well be.

Because he's right. If you aren't able to simply explain your area of expertise at a second grade-level, you don't understand it well enough.

And you definitely shouldn't be pitching it to the media.

Before you get upset and close this book, hear me out. In this chapter, I'll take you through exactly how you can pitch the media and standout in a crowded marketplace to get your target audience's attention.

WHAT IS A MEDIA PITCH

First, let's talk about what a media pitch actually is.

A media pitch is a suggested story idea that's submitted to its intended target by email. It gives the customer, reporter, or blogger an idea for a story. If the recipient likes the idea, they then write a story for their media outlet based on your suggestion.

And everybody wins!

By design, media pitches are shorter than a press release and more informative than marketing collateral.

Pitches also are better the more personalized you make each one. This attention to detail shows your contact that you've taken enough interest in them to get their name right, mention a previous article they've written, and are in tune with what's being covered by their media outlet.

WHY MEDIA PITCHES ARE IMPORTANT

Why are media pitches important?

A pitch is your way to tell your brand's story exactly as you would want it told to your targeted audience—including your key messages or elevator speech—by a trusted and respected third party.

A media pitch also is important because it:
- Shares your brand story with an audience you may not normally come in contact with
- Gives validity to your messages courtesy of the media outlet or third party promoter
- Aligns your brand with a point in time based on your pitch topic or subject
- Lets you set the tone for your brand by sharing your story, your way

While it's often thought of as intimidating or overwhelming, pitching the media doesn't have to be an intimidating or impossible task.

Your job is to figure out how to position your brand, product, or service so that the value to your target audience is crystal clear.

That's how easy drafting a pitch is!

THE DOS AND DON'TS

What are the dos of pitching?

When pitching, you should know not only your target audience, but also who you are reaching out to at each media outlet you are pitching.

You also should make it easy for the reporter or target customer to see exactly how what you're pitching will apply to them or make their lives easier.

Do this by giving them easy access to facts, images, and quotes to retell your story without hassle.

There also are some things you should not do when pitching the media or your target customers.

When pitching, you should not send out an email to any and all contacts.

You also should not email contacts at random without a point to your pitch or call to action.

And you definitely should not copy and paste the exact same pitch to all of your potential email contacts.

No matter what you do, do not share contact information for multiple people or media outlets by mass pitching and leaving their info on the To: line.

But don't let these dos and don'ts intimidate you!

If you know your audience, and make sure you are pitching the right contact and media outlet, you are golden.

Likewise, don't overthink it. Your media pitch isn't the be all and end all or the only shot you'll ever get to be featured in the media.

I promise you.

HURRY UP AND WAIT

Another important note I do want to share with you about pitching the media, is that you should be prepared to wait.

It's very rare that members of the media are sitting at their desks, waiting for a pitch to land in their inbox so they can immediately respond. Members of the media are understaffed, on deadlines, and often times covering a variety of industries.

When you send your pitch by email, wait two or three days before following up again. If you still haven't heard anything, reach out a third time by email. Or, gasp, by picking up the phone and calling your media contact to pitch your story idea.

FIVE TYPES OF PITCHES

Just like there's no one perfect way to eat ice cream, there's no one way to pitch your brand.

In fact, there are five different types of pitches to choose from. These include: Evergreen, seasonal, marketing holidays, newsjacked news, and promotional angles.

Evergreen media pitches
Just like evergreen trees, evergreen pitches are always in bloom and ready to go.

Evergreen pitches include topics that:
- Never lose relevance over time
- Endure despite fads and trends
- Always appear as fresh news to audience
- Have the great potential of all pitches to gain in popularity over time

Examples of evergreen pitches include:
- *Lists.* Aim for no more than top five or 10 list, however.
- *Tips.* Think dos and don'ts, as they're the most popular.
- *How tos.* How-to articles, with clear steps, are always a winner.

Evergreen content also can be shared in the form of infographics, images, and videos.

Seasonal media pitches
Another angle to take with your pitching is a seasonal approach.

Seasonal pitches include content that is tied in with specific holidays, events, or periods of time. They also include timely content that is easy to include in promotions.

What differentiates seasonal pitches from evergreen ones, is that season pitches have a limited window of opportunity and are best pitched in advance to ensure appropriate pickup.

Examples of seasonal pitches include:
- Traditional holidays like Halloween, Fourth of July, and New Year's Eve
- Stories focused on the actual seasons
- Any cultural references
- Clothing trends or related stories

Daylight Savings Time starting or ending is always a great seasonal pitch, no matter your industry.

Marketing holiday media pitches
A third type of angle to take when pitching is to focus on marketing holidays.

Based around days that exist purely for commercial or awareness purposes, marketing holidays do not commemorate a traditionally- or historically-significant event.

These days also can be repetitive, occurring on more than one day or even an entire week or month. But hey, I'm not mad that there are multiple National Donut Days every year!

What's great about marketing holidays is that there are literally thousands of them to choose from.

Examples of marketing holiday pitches include:
- Observances and important dates
- Stories focused on the lighthearted like National Wine or Best Friend Days
- Anything trending like celebrity birthdays, sporting events, or movie/album releases
- Sales like Black Friday or Cyber Monday

Marketing holidays apply to all ages and media outlets—from millennials on Instagram to Savannah and Hoda on *The Today Show.*

The later really love National Wine Day on May 25, by the way.

Newsjacked media pitches
Another type of pitch angle is Newsjacked pitches.

Newsjacked pitches are derived from the term newsjacking, which refers to something that happened locally, regionally, or nationally that sparks an idea that applies directly to your brand. You then take that topic and use it to bring attention to your brand or as a way to pitch your brand.

Examples of newsjacked pitches include:
- Krispy Kreme donuts using #deflategate news to promote that their football-shaped donuts were fully filled
- Cash for Purses "We'll Buy Your Purses, Lindsay!" Or when the company actually offered to pay big money for cash-strapped Lindsay Lohan's old handbags
- Encore Wynn Hotel waiving Prince Harry's £30,000 hotel bill and encouraging him to keep living like a king after photos of him in Vegas surfaced and threatened to ruin the hotel's reputation for keeping what happened in Vegas, not staying in Vegas

Just don't overdo it on your newsjacked media pitches. And, if you go with a newsjacked angle, make sure whatever you newsjack, you do in a tasteful way.

Promotional media pitches
The last type of pitch is the promotional pitch.

This type of media pitch is purely promotional in nature and is a way of letting your media contact be in the know ahead of anyone else. It rarely leads to a feature or coverage, but is useful after building rapport with your pitch's target recipient.

Examples of promotional pitches include:
- Sales and trend alerts from Zara and Target that appear on outlets like *Refinery29* and other female-friendly media outlets
- Anything Apple ever puts out publicly
- Prices of gas soaring news

This type of pitch angle sounds super salesy, because it is. Remember that. Don't make this type of pitch be your initial pitch to any contact at any time.

CHOOSING YOUR ANGLE

Not sure which angle is right for you or where to start?

Ask yourself these questions:
- What are the recent trends in my industry?
- What gaps in my industry does my brand fill that my competitors do not?
- Who benefits most from my offerings?
- What are the questions I am asked all the time by customers and potentials?

Still not sure what to pitch?

Kick-start your creativity with these angles:
- Connect your product to a current trend
- Show a celebrity in a look similar to yours
- Create a visual that connects your product to an upcoming or iconic film
- Pitch how your offerings are perfect for travel, business, or gifts
- Show your product as the perfect accessory for an event, like a music festival, first date, or even wedding

PUBLICITY PRACTICE

Now it's your turn to take action and apply the tips to get your pitch on!

Spend some time identifying which pitch angle applies best to your brand and PR goals and get started.

Don't worry if you have multiple pitches and angles to pursue. That's a good thing!

One word of caution, however, is that you really only need 12 pitches—one per month—to keep you busy and interacting with the media for an entire year. Make note of that.

CHAPTER TEN
NEWS-WORTHY NEWS RELEASES

We've covered a lot of ground in this book, from key messages to media pitches and even how marketing holidays can help populate your content calendar.

But we still haven't discussed one of the oldest PR tactics in operation, the news release.

I know what you're thinking.

"KJ, the news release is dead. How is this still relevant to PR?"

Well, you're wrong. And I'm extremely excited to chat you up about this PR tactic.

It may be an oldie, but it's still a goodie.

In this chapter, I'll walk you through exactly why the news release isn't dead and when you should still distribute one.

WHAT IS A NEW RELEASE

First, let's talk about what a news release is.

A news release is an official announcement that a brand issues to the media. This announcement also may be called a press release, press statement, or media release.

Most releases are succinct at just a page long. Or two pages, tops.

Ultimately, brands who issue news releases want to provide enough information so that media outlets have sufficient material for publishing their own stories about whatever the brand is announcing in the release.

While it may be tempting to draft a news release that embellishes your brand's accomplishments or twists the facts in your favor to make a story more intriguing, it's important to remember that news releases live in the public domain. Which means the public—including your customers and prospective customers—are able to view them.

So, instead of thinking of a news release as a ticket to earning news coverage, you should instead think of it as a valuable piece of marketing content. Part of your publicity strategy should include using news releases as an opportunity to connect to the audiences you care about.

Including, but not limited to, the media.

NEWS RELEASE RULES

Say you have an announcement in mind and want to know how to go about writing a press release. What do you do?

The first rule is to make your headline irresistible.

Just as you would work hard to write the perfect blog post title, you should set up your news release for success by choosing the right headline.

You only have one line to work with here, which can seem scary, but consider diction carefully to make your headline captivating.

Use action verbs, clear, understandable language, and keep your headline simple and short. After all, search engines reward the brief. So, keep your title to one line to clearly focus people's attention on your main message.

Most importantly, make your headline interesting: Keep in mind that members of the media receive dozens, if not hundreds, of releases each day.

Invest the time to write a compelling headline. It's worth the effort on your part.

The second rule of news releases is to not play hard to get. For reporters, influencers, or customers to be inclined to share your announcement, you must tell them upfront why they should care.

And how your news impacts them.

The first paragraph of your release should cover the who, what, why, where, and how of your new launch, update, or development.

The media doesn't have a ton of time to sift through details and fluffy background information. They need the facts fast that will help them tell your story to someone else from a position of authority.

For this reason, there shouldn't be any new, crucial information covered after this section that the reader could potentially miss.

The third rule of news releases is to offer a tempting quote.

Once you've set the scene in your release, it's time to bring your story to life with a quote that the media can use for context around your announcement which helps paint a picture of how your news affects the given industry, customer base, and landscape.

Ideally, quotes will be from key stakeholders in your company including your executive team, project leads, or those directly impacted by your announcement.

Why are quotes necessary? Because quoting key figures and authorities underlines the importance of your announcement. The chosen quote should shape your narrative and emphasize the key parts of your announcement.

Don't overdo it, though. Pick one or, at most, two critical spokespeople and focus the quotes around their unique perspective.

A fourth rule of news releases, is to provide valuable background information.

In this last paragraph, keep in mind that the reader already has all the vital details and information they need to file a story or spread the word about your news. It can be tempting to provide superfluous facts and tidbits about your brand; however, a news release needs to remain helpful and concise.

Offer details here that strengthen your narrative, like creative or noteworthy ways your company developed the project or announcement at hand. Or, when applicable, comment on future implications of your news.

The fifth and final rule of news releases is to make the who and what of each announcement extremely obvious.

Social media is full of media members lamenting PR contacts, releases, and pitches that don't clearly explain what the brand's news is or what the announcement is actually about.

Instead of being the butt of a reporter's joke, make your release incredible easy to reference.

Here are additional tips on creating a killer news release:
- Describe what your brand does in clear, plain English, without any jargon.
- Include a link to your brand's website early on, and make your boilerplate succinct and straightforward.
- If you cite data or any scientific studies, include a reference link for the source.
- Make sure every name in the release has an associated title as well.

To keep yourself honest on this front, ask a friend or peer to read your release without context and see if they can easily and readily explain why the news matters, what your brand is about, and why those quoted are included.

If the answer to any of those questions is no, go back and rewrite your announcement.

FOOL-PROOF FORMULA

Traditional news releases can still be extremely valuable when executed well.

Instead of ditching releases as a tactic, give them a modern makeover to make them more useful for your PR efforts.

While there's no cut-and-dried formula for when a news release should be written (or distributed), here are a few reasons when it's a good idea:
- New product launches
- Updates to existing products
- Opening a new office

- Introducing a new partnership
- Rebranding
- Promoting/hiring a new executive
- Receiving an award

A regular cadence of meaningful news can help your brand stand out and build mindshare with the media over time. This is where the news release comes in.

Many incorrectly assume that news releases must be full of buzzwords, five syllable jargon, and executive quotes that go on for multiple pages.

Instead of stuffing a release with any of these, apply a creative angle to help carry your content and increase the likelihood of social sharing.

By doing so, a news release can become a valuable medium for communicating news to your audiences.

As long as you ensure it is readable, relevant, and relatable.

NEWS RELEASE DISTRIBUTION

Writing a release is only half the battle. Once you're finished with its drafting, it's time to focus on distribution.

Of course, there are the traditional distribution levers we can pull, which include publishing the release on our website or blog, as well as sharing the news with our followers on social media and subscribers by email.

However, to ensure your release gets the maximum amount of distribution possible, here are some tips you can follow:

1. Reach out to a specific media contact instead of blasting the release out to every media contact you can find an email address for.

By focusing on a few key contacts who have experience covering your industry (and brand, hopefully) and sending them a personalized message, you ensure your news will receive more coverage.

Remember to connect the dots and show why your news connects to what they write.

2. Don't be afraid to go offline. Most media contacts have mountains of emails (and news releases) to sort through.

   Try sending your release through another channel, like a wire distribution service or an attention-grabbing media kit, to differentiate yourself. And make sure it gets seen.

3. Send your release to key contacts the day prior. Give your targets extra time to write a story around your news by sending it to them under embargo the day before it officially goes live.

   Under embargo simply means they aren't allowed to share the information in the release until the time you specify.

4. To avoid competition, don't hit publish on your release on the hour.

   If you're publishing your release on a wire distribution service like PRWeb, PR Newswire or Business Wire, avoid publishing it on the hour like one o'clock or three o'clock and instead publish it at a more distinct time, such as 8:12 am, 1:18 pm, or 5:25 pm.

   The reason? Most schedule their releases to go out on the hour, which means if yours does too, it's likely to get lost in the shuffle.

5. Share your coverage. If all goes according to plan, your release will get picked up by the media.

   Guess what? This means your job isn't finished. To keep the buzz going, release a second wave of distribution by sharing the specific stories that news outlets write based on your release across all your other channels—including social media, your blog, your email list, and more.

PUBLICITY PRACTICE

Now it's your turn to take action and apply the tips in this chapter to your brand.

Spend some time thinking over what you'd like to say in your news release. Then, take action by getting to work and writing it down.

Don't worry if the copy for your release doesn't come to you immediately. The key is for you to start brainstorming and getting your ideas down on paper. Even the professionals who have been writing releases for years go through multiple edits before they distribute their news.

CHAPTER ELEVEN
PR TOOLS TO USE

We've reach the point in the book where I start to feel a little like Oprah.

You get a free PR tool! And you get a free PR tool! Everyone gets a free PR tool!

If you've followed along with this book this far, you know I love sharing tips and tools for how you can achieve all your publicity dreams.

This chapter is no different.

Within these pages, we'll be discovering the free tools and resources available to help your brand become a media darling in no time.

Without costing you a penny.

Because the world of PR should be magical, not an impossible mystery only those with unlimited budgets can navigate.

HELP A REPORTER OUT (HARO)

Known primarily by the acronym of HARO, Help a Reporter Out provides you with real-time media opportunities up to three times daily that come straight from journalists on a deadline who need a source. You can find this amazing resource at helpareporter.com.

What's great about HARO, is that you can filter opportunities by industry and start submitting your info immediately wherever it is relevant. These are eager to cover you media contacts ready and willing to use your quote submissions verbatim.

I've had clients featured in *Forbes*, *Inc.*, *Martha Stewart*, *Real Sim*ple, *Southern Living*, Brit + Co, *USA Today*, Oprah's Favorite Things, and so many others simply by responding to a HARO inquiry.

Taking advantage of free PR resources available should be the first stop for anyone looking to get published. And for this, I can't recommend HARO enough.

ONEPITCH

Like HARO, OnePitch is a newer email pitch platform that matches your media pitches to journalists' preferences through a specific categorization and vetting process.

Once pitches have been submitted, OnePitch sends one email a day of the pitches that matches the exact topics and industries selected by journalists. Those same journalists then have the option to contact the person responsible for that pitch directly if desired.

What's great about OnePitch is that from start to finish, you control your story and what is submitted on your behalf to journalists. It's exactly like pitching the media by email—but better, because OnePitch has already sourced media contacts interested in industries like yours that are eager for news.

Visit onepitch.co to learn more or sign up for this service.

ANEWSTIP

Have you ever wondered how you could search for tweets, news articles, media contacts, and media outlet profiles in one fell swoop when Google fails you?

Anewstip is your answer.

This free resource features an influence score and lets you filter by time, topic, or language. Plus, the tool features alerts and media lists.

You can find this resource at anewstip.com.

#JOURNOREQUEST

While it may not technically be a PR tool, per say, I do refer to this hashtag as my publicity secret weapon.

Meet #journorequest. It'll be your new best friend, too.

Use #journorequest the next time you hop on Twitter, as it's the hashtag used by the media when they are looking for contributors, experts, or quotes.

GOOGLE ALERTS

Don't be that person that puts in tons of effort to get media attention and then doesn't keep track of the fruits of their labor. No one likes that person.

Instead, use Google Alerts!

This free service will track mentions of your brand across the web. And, it even ensures that you won't miss a mention by providing easy-to-customize email alerts.

If you don't feel like Googling the answer, google.com/alerts will take you right to the alert setup.

DROPBOX

It's the 21st Century and media contacts don't open attachments any longer.

I swear, it's true!

If you have more than just a link to share, your new best friend is Dropbox. This is the perfect resource for sharing multiple file formats and not clogging up a reporter's inbox.

I use Dropbox for everything from media kits to influencer forms to image sharing and more.

You can get yours setup at dropbox.com.

BANANATAG

If you're anything like me, sometimes you just have no chill.

Especially when pitching.

If you truly can't wait and want to know if someone has opened your email (without aggressively badgering them), sign up for BananaTag.

This service has a free option, which gives you 10 free email trackings per day, as well as a variety of paid packages that vary in pricing.

Another great benefit of this platform is email scheduling, which allows you to write pitch emails in advance and schedule them out for another date.

You can learn more at bananatag.com.

ANSWER THE PUBLIC

Not sure what you should be pitching or what questions your target audience is looking for answers to around your specific industry?

Give Answer the Public, a search query data visualization tool that fetches and maps keyword suggestions and predictions, a try.

Simply visit answerthepublic.com and enter a keyword in the search. You'll be presented with questions, prepositions, and alphabetical lists related to your query.

As you can see, getting PR going for your brand doesn't have to be expensive or a challenge.

Start using even just one of the free options above, and you'll see the buzz around your brand increase.

PUBLICITY PRACTICE

Are you ready to give these freebies a spin? Now it's your turn to take action and research the resources mentioned in this chapter.

Some may, or may not, apply to your brand. But looking into the ones that appeal to you is definitely worth your time.

Plus, they're free! How can you not love that?

CHAPTER TWELVE
PERFECT PRESS PAGES

Before we dive into this chapter, I need to start by stating the following: A press page is a powerful way to showcase your expertise.

If you do it right.

That's what I'll be walking you through in this section of the book—press page basics and how to use this simple webpage to your advantage.

First, we're going to take a few minutes to explain just how easy it is to set up a press page that gets you noticed. The best part is, you already have all the tools and technology at your fingertips—no additional fees, services, or staff required.

WHAT IS A PRESS PAGE

By definition, a press page is a place for you to show-off.

Typically a single page added on to your website, a press page acts as a central repository for all media coverage, press mentions, social media mentions, and other shoutouts you've been getting in the online media.

It also serves as a central hub for any images, logos, or other information you want to provide to the media who are interested in sharing your story with ease.

WHY IT'S NECESSARY

Let's say that you just wrapped up an incredible successful PR campaign.

You're thrilled, but when it starts to pick up media attention, it becomes very clear that you're unprepared.

The media and other influencers are looking to report on the story you've been pitching, but are having a hard time getting a hold of you, and when they do, you find that you're fumbling around trying to piece together the assets they need to finalize their stories.

So, instead of tons of attention on your brand, your efforts have resulted in nothing.

Whomp, whomp.

The truth is, this is an entirely preventable mess.

Having a clean, informative press page is invaluable because it aims to simplify the process of discovery by making it easy for outside sources—especially the media— to publicly recognize your brand.

When creating an effective page, the goal is to anticipate everything the media might need.

WHAT TO INCLUDE

Here's a primer on what you should include on your press page.

You know the phrase, content is king?

Well, on your press page, contact information is king. And it should be easy to spot.

No questions asked.

At the very least, you'll want to supply people with the phone number or email address of whomever is in charge of handling media requests for the brand.

While factors like company size and industry may influence how much information you are at liberty to give away, feel free to also list the name or names of those in charge of inquiries, a mailing address, and information specific about any additional locations.

The focus here is to provide just the right amount of detail without sacrificing clarity and length.

Essentially, you want visitors to be able to quickly and easily grasp what it is that the your brand does or stands for without any confusion or need for further clarification.

Here are a few fundamental elements that you should aim to include:
- When the brand was founded
- Who is involved in the brand, including founders, investors, and the like
- What services or products the brand offers
- Office locations
- Size of your company
- Any noteworthy growth statistics

If you're looking to provide more context, consider presenting additional information in the form of a timeline. This is an effective format for those looking to extract quick bits of information and gain a better understanding of the brand's story.

Have you recently been interviewed or quoted in the media? Has your brand received any awards or nominations? What about a mention in a noteworthy publication?

Any and all of these instances are worth linking to on the press page, as detailing media coverage helps to position the brand as both credible and newsworthy.

Personally, I love the idea of presenting your recent media features in a clean, organized list called out by media outlet logos and then links directly to the article or feature. Recognizable visuals help to capture the attention of those scanning the page for quick hits.

And, I don't know about you, but I love a good eye-catching moment.

As we discuss in a previous video, news releases are commonly thought to be long, buttoned-up documents riddled with buzzwords; however, that's not always the case. Your press page is a great place to post your announcements as they are both informative and easily digestible for the audience craving more info on you.

At a glance, visitors can scroll down the page to check out headlines accompanied by an image and a brief explanation of the announcement.

When a media source goes to write something up about a brand, it will first need to get its hands on a few important assets—including images, bios, social media links, and more.

To eliminate back and forth requests, your press page should serve as a hub for the following things:

- *Logos.* You may want to include several different variations of the company's logo. For example, many brands have both a dark version of their logo as well as a lighter variation that can be used to ensure contrast and optimal visibility when placed against different backgrounds.
- *Screenshots.* If your brand offers an app or software, or is digitally-based, clear, up-to-date screenshots are a critical piece of the puzzle. Don't be shy about how many different views you include—the more views, the merrier.
- *Headshots and bios.* At the very least, you want to include high quality headshots and current bios for any of the brand's founders, executives, and key team members. Links to their social media accounts are helpful, too.
- *Office photos.* These are of lesser importance than the assets listed above, but it's not uncommon for people to go looking for office photos to use as a featured image or within an article. Remember, as humans, we are voyeurs and we want to know everything about and feel like we are a part of a brand we admire.

PUBLICITY PRACTICE

Ready to have a press page that's the envy of the World Wide Web?

Start brainstorming articles, images, and other assets you can include to make your press page an easy one stop shop for the media.

If you get stuck, fire up your computer and scroll around to see how other brands—or your competitors—lay out their press pages.

CHAPTER THIRTEEN
PROMOTING YOU PR

Now that we have your press page dialed in and you're poised for greatness, it's time we had a chat about the best way to publicize your media placements.

How?

By using tips and tricks to help extend your fifteen minutes of fame through engaging and fun content.

Because, congratulations! You were just featured in the media.

So now what do you do?

Well, once you've received media coverage, it's time to promote your own PR.

TOOT YOUR HORN

I can almost hear you saying, "But wait, KJ. What does that even mean?"

It means it is time to extend your 15 minutes of fame in a strategic way to further your brand recognition. It also is an exercise in making your media coverage work its hardest for you.

While it might sound complicated, promoting your own PR is actually very easy.

For instance, I was recently featured on a podcast discussing PR tips for influencers and bloggers.

Using this example as a guide, I want to talk you through six examples of how you can promote your PR.

GET SOCIAL

First, you need to get social.

You can do this by promoting the article, mention, or feature across all your social media accounts.

That's right, no matter which platform or channel it is, share from your personal, business, brand, and even your dog's social media accounts.

What's great about this activity, is that you can post that day, the following day, or even weeks later.

In fact, if you follow me on Instagram (hint: @kjblattenbauer), you know that I love to share any media opportunity from every account and angle available to me.

Hey, if you can't toot your own horn, who's going to toot it for you?

Remember, being featured in the media isn't just a one-off occurance. It's evergreen content that keeps on giving and will always be relevant to your audience.

Now and years from now.

And, as you'll remember from a previous chapter, evergreen content is pretty amazing to have at your disposal, isn't it?

Plus, for you shy folks, it's not really bragging if you're merely sharing the kind word-of-mouth praise others have said about you.

Now is it?

I can almost see you nodding in agreement while you're reading this.

BLOG IT OUT

Another way to extend your fifteen minutes of fame, is to write about it.

Let's face it, people are busy. Not everyone who loves your brand is going to see every post about you. Likewise, not everyone remembers everything they only read once.

Repetition is key. So, be repetitive.

See what I did there?

Draft a blog post about the experience of being featured. Include the link to the media you've received. If possible, include an image of your product or brand being featured.

You don't have to be super creative or go crazy here. The point is just to reshare.

Guess what? You're currently reading a chapter in a book that is promoting the media hit I was recently featured in right now.

See how easy that was to promote my own PR?

GIVE THANKS

You know the saying, gratitude is the right attitude?

It holds true in promoting your PR, too.

The same manners you were taught about sending a handwritten thank you note after an interview or meeting, also apply to media coverage and brand love.

Make sure you send a kind note or thank you to the editor you worked with.

And, where appropriate—which is everywhere—copy or tag the source who helped you secure this media coverage or featured you.

I go out of my way to tag and mention those who helped by giving me brand love everywhere it is possible.

This not only helps give them the warm fuzzies, but also encourages them to reshare your post or mention. Which in turn, gets you in front of more people.

Aren't you thankful this type of kindness is the publicity gift that keeps on giving?

PAGE YOURSELF

Where do you direct almost every one of your customers or potential customers? To your website!

Does your site have a press page section for you to feature your media coverage, press hits, or features with a note that says "as seen in"?

It should.

I mean, it is the entire purpose of this part of this book, right?

In fact, you should update your site every time one of your offerings or your brand is featured. And, if you're featured multiple times in one day on a station, include a link to every single clip!

There is no shame in your press page game. Nor is there such a thing as press page overkill.

Trust me on this.

Again, I can't stress this enough: The reality of the situation is, if you aren't promoting yourself, no one else will.

Get a press page on your website today!

SPREAD THE WORD

Finally, you need to spread the word.

You know that email list you've spent so much time building?

The day after you secure media coverage is the perfect time to reach out to the fans, followers, and friends on your list.

Send out an email blast to customers, potential clients, wholesalers, and other contacts with the news.

Include the direct link to the article, image, or video when you can.

Make is easy for those on your list to share your exciting news by including a sample tweet, post, or by forwarding on your email in its entirety.

It's not spamming anyone if they've opted in to your mailing list. They signed up because they want to hear from you and are big fans of yours.

Give the people what they're asking for! Send. That. Email.

ALERT THE MEDIA

Finally, I don't care how big your brand is, when a celebrity wears, uses, or endorses you, it's a big deal.

Alert the media!

Literally, I'm begging you to let the media know, okay?

If a celebrity is photographed wearing or using your product, and that photograph shows up in one of the many celebrity weeklies or celeb style blogs, it's possible for the image to receive millions of views. The level of public interest can, though not always, have a significant, immediate impact on sales.

Get your hands on that photograph (include proper photo credit always) and promote this publicity the same way you would a news article or TV segment using the tips above.

Send a short pitch, featuring this celebrity sighting to your media connections. Particularly those with a celebrity focus.

Don't forget to also send the image to current wholesalers and potential retailers. They like to see the reach your brand can get, too.

And, tell your customers about it. Whether via your email list or on social media. When a celebrity is repping your brand, others want to rep the exact same thing, too.

And you don't hate making sales, now do you?

PUBLICITY PRACTICE

Whew! We covered a lot of ground in this chapter.

But, it's all easily implementable tasks that you can start today that will have a huge impact on your brand's buzz moving forward.

So don't delay! Get started on brainstorming ways you can promote your past, current, and future media opportunities.

Because the only bad media hit is the one you're not promoting, right?

CHAPTER FOURTEEN
MEDIA KIT MAGIC

Pop quiz time!

What's the number one thing that will make you stand out to potential collaborators and the media alike?

Two words: Media kit.

Whether you're new on the scene as a brand or blogger, and even if you're a seasoned veteran, having a polished and professional media kit will give you an edge over the competition and help outside parties realize your value.

But, before you dive into this chapter, I want to give it to you straight: It does take a bit of time investment to put a great-looking media kit together. Once it's done, however, you'll have it for the rest of your brand's life.

Look, friend, your media kit doesn't have to be some terrifying project.

It's actually pretty simple.

Just a few quick steps and you're done.

So as soon as you are finished reading this chapter, promise me you'll get after creating yours?

Awesomesauce. Let's dive in to all things media kits, shall we?

MEDIA KITS EXPLAINED

First, let's get real on what a media kit is.

A media kit, also known as a press kit, is a document that contains resources and information for the media and brands.

Do you need a media kit? Of course you do!

This PR tool makes it easy to quickly learn about you (or your brand), and access any photos and/or marketing materials that can be of use.

By providing a media kit, you're saying, "Hey, my brand loves press! Here's everything you need to put your story together as well as how to reach me."

Or, if you're an influencer, "Hey, I love collaborating! Here's everything you need to know to work with me ASAP."

WHY MEDIA KITS MATTER

For influencers, a media kit is an amazing tool for communicating with sponsors and brands you want to collaborate with.

It also shows them you know what you are doing. And are a professional.

For brands, a media kit also is an amazing tool because it's like a resume for your brand. Your kit is your best foot forward, professionally-speaking, that will help weed out media attention or collaborations that aren't a good match for you or are a waste of your time.

And let's be real, who really has extra time to waste these days?

MEDIA KIT CONTENTS

What goes into a media kit?

You might think it's just dry, boring facts like your Google Analytics stats and your pricing, but if you stop there, you're selling yourself short.

A media kit is an opportunity to show off your brand's best features—like it's personality, style, and what makes your offerings unique.

The key elements of a brand's media kit are similar to the press page on your website. Remember we discussed that in a previous chapter?

Similar ideas apply here and include:
- A traditional news release or feature-style article about the brand
- An interesting interview or Q&A with bio information on the company founder
- A few images that tell a visual story about the brand
- Product images against a white background, available at high- and low-res
- Recent, noteworthy media coverage that is less than six months old
- Contact information and social media links

Extra bonus points if you make this information easy to download and reuse.

For an influencer, the key elements of a media kit are:
- A headshot or collage of 3-4 images that showcase your brand
- A brief 100-word or less bio about you
- A brief 100-word or less bio about your blog
- All your social media outlets and stats
- Mentions of recent collaborations
- Your pricing for every service you offer
- Contact information and social media links

Remember when I mentioned it only takes a few steps to create a media kit?

I just walked you through the first one, gathering your resources.

This is the biggest, and most time-consuming, hurdle to get over, but once you have everything you need in one place, it'll give you momentum to finish the job.

Let's walk through the rest now!

NAIL YOUR INTRO

A key part of your media kit is going to be your introduction.

Since the introduction is the first thing people will see when they read your media kit, make it count.

Remember that elevator speech we worked on in an earlier video? You're going to want to put that bad boy to work here.

There's plenty of space for your statistics, but you need to make your introduction personal. Tell a little bit about yourself or your brand—whatever shows the real you.

You also will want to put a photo here. Not a long-range image but a face-to-face greeting that shows how friendly you are or how great your product or service is.

If your work has been featured in any magazines, books, well-known blogs or other publications, here's where to tell about it.

It doesn't have to be long; a simple "featured in _____" will do.

STATS AND MORE

Another great addition to your media kit will be presenting your statistics and accomplishments.

Here's where you'll use all those fun numbers. Because who doesn't like big numbers, right?

From a brand standpoint, this is an excellent spot to include numbers like:
- Years you've been in business
- Annual sales or net worth
- Social media stats

At the very least, as an influencer, you should include your:
- Unique visitors per month
- Page views per month
- Subscribers (RSS and mailing list, if you have one)

It's important to make sure that you stay current with your stats. In fact, you can even put "current as of [date]" and then make sure that date is within the last three months.

It's not helpful to give your numbers from further out than that because, as you know, a lot can happen in over a few months.

So always keep it current.

Aside from the three items above, if there are any numbers you *don't* feel are impressive, just leave them out.

Sorry, your 12 Facebook followers don't need to make the cut.

What if you're just starting out? Or you don't have impressive numbers?

Don't sweat it, friend.

If you don't have impressive numbers to show off, think about including your growth trends.

For example, if you've only had a blog for a few months, yet in the last week grew your email subscriptions by 500 percent, include that stat instead.

It's impressive!

The same holds true for brands.

If you aren't a million-dollar company, but you recently tripled your wholesalers or great your revenue by double, include those facts.

They matter, because it shows you know what you're doing.

NOTE TO INFLUENCERS

Now influencers, this one is just for you.

Because I hear a lot of conflicting advice out there and I want to be very clear with you on where I stand about pricing and including it in your media kit.

Include your pricing in your media kit!

No one has time for 900 emails back and forth over what you're going to charge for an Instagram post.

That's silly. Not to mention a huge waste of everyone's time.

Just as what you're receiving in payment is important to you, it is important to point out to your potential sponsors what they'll be getting out of the deal.

Here are some things you need to consider for your collaborations with sponsors:

- What are your rates? If you offer different options for paid promotions or collaborations, list the price out for each. The larger the time commitment on your end, the higher the price.
- Do you offer your sponsors the opportunity for a giveaway? If so, these almost always come with special terms—like an extra fee, or a certain number of months of sponsorship before they're eligible to offer a giveaway.
- Do you conduct product reviews? Brands are probably aware that the most powerful kind of advertising is an in-post link that flows naturally from the context of your writing. So it's okay to state that while you consider giveaways and reviews that fit with your topic and your readership, if they want the star sponsor treatment, samples must be provided by the sponsor.
- Outline any payment policies, such as payment being required within a certain time frame prior to the month of sponsorship. Also give details of when the images are due to you and what file types you accept (just JPGs and GIFs, or do you allow animated buttons, too?).

These are all important factors to consider, but as you're thinking about them, remember that if you want to find a sponsorship match made in heaven, you have to be a great collaborator first.

GET FEEDBACK

Next, you're going to want to gather some testimonials.

You can talk all day long about how great your brand is or what an amazing opportunity it is to collaborate with you. However, getting other people to promote you is priceless.

It's not that other people will say things you couldn't say yourself, but it means more coming from others.

It's third-party validation and technically, the entire point of PR.

Having great testimonials alone on your side won't convince sponsors to collaborate with you or the media to cover you, but great recommendations will help solidify your worth as an influencer or brand.

Which, in turn, boosts your credibility and chances at success.

If you don't already have testimonials in hand, it's time to reach out and ask for some. If it makes you feel uncomfortable, buckle up because it's time for some tough love.

In fact, it's time to get over asking for what you need.

Besides, how are you ever going to get what you want if you're too afraid to ask for it?

CALL TO ACTION

Now it's time to wrap it up!

It would be a shame to make it this far in your media kit dealings and not remind to remember the all-important call to action at the end.

Give your potential sponsors or media contacts their next steps.

How can they get in touch with you? Leave your contact information front and center.

And don't write "To find out more about sponsorship" or "For more information about our brand," because that's what they've just done in reading your media kit.

Rather, include something more along the lines of:

To begin sponsorship with [your brand's name], please contact [name of contact] at [email address].

Or even, To interview [your brand's key executive], please contact [name of contact] at [email address].

So that's it!

Almost.

The writing portion is done. The only thing left is to tie it up in a bow.

Before you send your media kit anywhere, and this includes uploading it to your site, please PDF your document.

Ta-dah! Your work here is done.

You now have a shiny new media kit ready to send out to the media or potential sponsors.

How cool is that?

PUBLICITY PRACTICE

What are you waiting for?

Head on over to Cavna or fire up your favorite graphic design tool and start making your very own media kit!

Spend some time identifying which assets and information mention in this chapter best to your brand and PR goals. Leave out what isn't a good fit for you.

One word of caution, however, is that you really only one to two pages in your media kit. Anything additional is kind of overkill.

BONUS CHAPTER
MEDIA PITCH TEMPLATES

These email swipe will help you draft a clear, concise, and response-worthy pitch for collaborations.

Simply fill in the blanks, customize the language to fit your voice, and then hit send!

GENERAL INTRO PITCH

Hello [contact's name],

I hope you are doing well. I'm a big fan of your [blog, outlet, social media page, etc.] and especially loved your [specific article or feature]. I'm a [share info about you and your story here in a sentence or two max].

I wanted to share our brand story [or newest offering] with you, which I know your readers will love. Some benefits you can expect with it are:
* [Benefit one]
* [Benefit two]

- [Benefit three]

Our offering is [list two to three features of your offering that make it unique]. It retails for [price here], and can be purchased on [your website].

Please let me know if you would like more information or hi-res images. I'm happy to send either your way.

Thank you,

[Your name and contact information]

[Your contact information, including social media handles, website, email, and phone number so they can reach our or research you]

GENERAL BRAND PITCH

Hello [contact's name],

I loved your story on [insert story title]. [Insert one sentence on why you loved the story].

I have a brand that I would love to get on your radar: [brand name hyperlink to website], based out of [city]. Since launching [launch date], [brand name] has experienced [xx% growth or has done $$ in sales].

[1-lines on what the brand does/provides. 1-2 lines on what makes the brand unique or special.]

Some notables for the company include: [milestones, 1-2].

[Founder name] is a [line on background of founder].

Other interesting facts: [1-2 interesting tidbits about the brand and its journey so far].

Thank you,

[Your name and contact information]

[Your contact information, including social media handles, website, email, and phone number so they can reach our or research you]

NEW OFFERING PITCH

Hello [contact's name],

I hope this email finds you well. I loved your recent story on [insert story title].

I wanted to fill you in on the latest offering from [brand], which is [basic offering description].

[Line further describing offering]. [Line on inspiration behind the offering].

Available at [hyperlinked URL], [offering name] retails for [price].

Would love for you to consider coverage of [offering name]. Please let me know if I can provide samples, imagery, or additional information.

Thank you,

[Your name and contact information]
[Your contact information, including social media handles, website, email, and phone number so they can reach our or research you]

OFFERING REVIEW PITCH

Hello [contact's name],

I know you're super busy, so I'll keep this short. My name is [your name] from [brand name]. We developed an offering that makes [solution: x more affordable, easy to use, functional, etc. but focus on the benefit]. I definitely think it's something you (and your readers) might be interested in. [Add in one single sentence describing your offering and its connection to this contact].

We're at [your website link], and I have a sample I'd love to send your way to checkout or review if you'd be interested. Please let me know!

Thank you,

[Your name and contact information]

[Your contact information, including social media handles, website, email, and phone number so they can reach our or research you]

NEW OFFERING PITCH

Hello [contact's name],

I hope this email finds you well. I loved your recent story on [insert story title].

I wanted to fill you in on the latest offering from [brand], which is [basic offering description].

[Line further describing offering]. [Line on inspiration behind the offering].

Available at [hyperlinked URL], [offering name] retails for [price].

Would love for you to consider coverage of [offering name]. Please let me know if I can provide samples, imagery, or additional information.

Thank you,

[Your name and contact information]

[Your contact information, including social media handles, website, email, and phone number so they can reach our or research you]

GUEST POST PITCH

Hello [contact's name],

I've been following your blog for quite some time, and I love your content and what you share with your followers. Every time I read a post, I feel like I'm able to take a single, clear lesson away from it, which is why I think it's so great. One example that really resonated with me is, [mention content and how it impacted you].

I'm reaching out to see if you'd be interested in featuring a guest post from me. I'm [briefly mention who you are, what you do, and why this is relevant for this blog and its readers].

I believe I can add value to your audience on a few different topics. I've included a few proposed
ones I think would resonate with your readers here:
- [Proposed title or topic]
- [Proposed title or topic]
- [Proposed title or topic]

Please let me know if you'd be interested in learning more or partnering.

Thank you,

[Your name and contact information]

[Your contact information, including social media handles, website, email, and phone number so they can reach our or research you]

GENERAL COLLAB PITCH

Hello [Name of contact],

My name is [your name], and I'm the voice behind [name of your blog (and hyperlink it)].

I've been a big fan of [their product or company] for [number of years] years, and love what you're doing with [insert specific product, service, or campaign of brand's].

As a fan, I'd love to help promote your cause. [Provide one or two sentences on how you can help further promote their advertising mission with your influencer status.]

Please let me know if you are interested in working together.

Thank you,

[Your name]

[Your contact information, including social media handles, website, email, and phone number so they can reach our or research you]

* Don't forget to attach or link your media kit!

CONCLUSION

Congratulations! You did it, friend. You've finished this entire book and can call yourself a Media Darling.

Definitely celebrate because finishing what you start is such an accomplishment. But, do not think this is the end of your publicity journey. Because, it's not.

In fact, it is just the beginning!

Let's face it, this is where the real fun begins because you have the insight, wisdom, and tools necessary to be a huge success at getting press. From here on out, it's all about execution.

And execution is everything!

But you're a go-getter, so I know you already know this.

Insight without action is worthless. But don't just take any action.

Take the strategic and purposeful action we've discussed throughout this book.

1. *Know exactly what you want.* Clarity is power and you've already outlined your goals.
2. *Know exactly what you want to say.* You have the information and how to share it at your fingertips. Promote your messages!
3. *Execute.* Get focused, be committed, and get to work!
4. *Pay attention.* Look at what's working and what is not working. It's all a learning experience. All about progress, not perfection.
5. *Use this feedback.* Adjust your publicity strategy as necessary based on the feedback you're receiving.

And definitely don't forget this: You are not alone.

Truthfully, I'm here for you! Reach out at any time on Instagram.

Look, I know it can be scary promoting your brand. And I know it can be scary putting yourself out there. But, you can come back as often as you'd like and take your PR game to the next level by reading this book again. And I'll be with you every step of the way.

Now, as our time together comes to an end in this format, I have one last favor to ask of you: Please, treat yourself with kindness and grace.

If you're anything like I am, then you have big dreams and you've got super high standards. Which probably means you can be really hard on yourself. So promise me that you'll respect yourself and go at a pace that allows yourself grace.

Thank you so much for allowing me the honor and privilege to serve as your guide on your publicity journey. Please keep me posted on your progress. And send me updates.

Seriously, I can't wait to see your name in the media!

With all my love and gratitude, thank you again for choosing this book, and me.

Good bye for now, friend!

Printed in Great Britain
by Amazon

63302480R00078